CANTUS
Table of Contents

*

*

*

*

INTRODUCTION
CANTUS

Why "Cantus"? Cantus, the word, in Latin means "song", a reference to the poetic affiliation of Canto... This is my own song, and hopefully it belongs in the hearts of humankind. The title was written in the supposed "dead language" of Latin- that is deceptively very much alive and influential in modern languages. It was once a universal language and continues to permeate our communication today. I use Latin in naming my premier book, akin to science in naming species in the interest to use a global language in identification. These elements of life are out there for our perceiving which then leads to a higher meaning. These words are not a directive to take a stance, rather to take to a movement.

Why Cantus? The reason for writing this book has much to do with my inclination since age 13 to write poetry. The words came first, then very shortly after- the meaning. Then the importance set in. Now, I feel the imperative to share it with anyone who will be able to stop in their busy daily life and enter into something deeper. What importance am I to my community or generation or the aeons of those preceding or following? Good question. I do not know. But I can say this is important and I believe it enriches all who contemplate its depths.

These poems are meditations as well as songs. I sing them and at once I both treasure them for their elemental human rhythms and release them to an audience. This book is a reflection. There is a greater reality than what any one person can capture, but this text is an introduction into the greater part of our lives than we often neglect. It is a step forward in that pursuit. When you

*

read "I" or "You" in the text, consider yourself on both sides. Ultimately an indictment to one is a call for accountability to all. Surely, I do not presume to be greater than my own perspective, yet I feel a gift to formulate these words and an imperative to introduce this to you and simultaneously responsibility for myself.

My style is concise and direct, my words are strictly intentional- so you will not be panning for what I think is gold. I will offer to you my thought and you can trust that there is much to be examined in that text. I may from time to time offer a short journey, but that too is to serve a strict purpose- to arrive to an idea.

So in the deliberation over what here I write... take it in slowly. You be the judge once you consider this: process but a few poems in one reading. Unless you feel a connectedness that flows, that permeating contemplation- then, by all means, continue on. I offer my email troika7@gmail.com for questions and discussion.

Curiosity holds the beauty of discovery and positions one for learning which is more fruitful than those who have preconceived notions. I list titles which were named in reference to a specific line or phrase in the poem, as to not impose an idea. Listen. Cantus.

*

Black crow
Blue night
Caw
Gawk
Flock…
        Less
Flies in circles

*

In quitting,
    One lays one's power down
    To weakness
The power exists
But the weak
    Have lost recognition

*

Delving deeper into one's self
    Polarizes
The depths of one's self
    Determine the righteousness
    Of such an act

*

I know we defame
        What we do not understand
In absentia
But I am here
        And I am clear
It is not of good use

She fills
    Every sense in every word
Dedicated to the one I love:
    Johanna
Dedicated to Johanna
    The one I love
To Johanna
The Johanna
One- Johanna
Dedicated to the Johanna I love
Dedicated to the one,
    Johanna, Love
Love Johanna
    My love is Johanna
Dedicated to the one I Johanna
I- Johanna
One.

*

Life is a lesson
In how to learn

*

Spontaneous reaction
Kills the messenger

*

At this address no more
At one time parenting
    To raise this daughter
    To culpability
To protect her
    But allow struggle
    To teach
His dynasty remains in her blue eyes
And her quiet peace

In the desert,
    The parched sand
Indicative of my throat
In the forest,
    Moisture pooled on my tongue-
    Akin to the leaves
The sea...
    The sea deceived me

*

Your limitations-
Your cross
But your attitude
Is your crucifixion

*

Dismiss all knowledge
By accepting all beliefs

*

Embrace others' deficiencies
    To handicap yourself with excuse
Reformulate oxymoron
    Into reciprocal terms
Avoiding answers
Fornicating with contentment
Recluse- to hide and never seek
    Prove me wrong
    Prove anything right
In guise of a prophet

*

Inundate you with love
For by a chance moment
Regressed
A moment remiss

*

Everyone
    Has holes in their thinking
Evermore in their speaking
Our dubious task is
    To not fall inside

*

Practice as if
      An underdog
Play as
      The champion

*

The counselor should be architect
Collaborating with the client,
    The construction worker
Erroneous for the counselor
To interfere
    As the construction worker
Turning the client into
    The inanimate project

*

Mankind is full of desire
What are we, if not loyal?
New desire breeds of
New mutiny

*

One exclaims,
        'Tonight is not as dark as last night'
The other glibs,
        'Even Hell has firelight'
Some are afraid
        Of another's cognition
But I say,
        How many are afraid of their own?

*

Whether in reference
  Of behind, or
  In front of
The sun
We are speaking
    Geocentrically

*

There was change within me
When I was with you
But there was no change within you,
When with me
I rose and
Conceived of things
While you allowed things
Contrive you

*

Virtue-
   None sought
Your advice-
   Dead to me
Your efforts-
   An epitaph

*

Enemies introduce anger
Inside you
There it dwells
And is used
To destroy you

*

To understand emptying
To understand humility
    We cannot visit once
But visit again and again
To learn
    Again and again

*

You may plant or eat
The seed
Depending on the urgency
Of need

*

Chased illusion
So long
It became delusion
When can we ever
Be for certain
We move by whim

*

I have walked the lengths
Of bohemia
And Sparta
Found the middle ground
More profound

*

With an ounce of anger
And pound of retribution
You are unsatisfied
Such things still
    Weigh on you

*

How many times we throw things
        To the sky
Forgetting the fallout
The highest
        One can throw
        With any given effort
Is directly up
So it returns
        Upon our head

*

The wise man
      Has much to learn
The fool
      Is full of knowledge

*

Ability falls to will
It matters not of the examination
    But of the heart-
    Examine it
I care
    But can't obsess
I do
    But don't excess
Got a little piece of Heaven
    But can't explain

*

Mad at my size
Mole hills eventuate
        Into mountains
This is the Truth as I see it
        And if unfettered- my sight
This is Truth
I refer to blindness
        Not in physical terms
For the sightlessness
        Is not the blind man's burden
Inclined to insight
Our obligations staggering
        Studied from afar

*

Be strong in wretchedness
Not assured in righteousness
Nor defeated
There is a path
    In which we are all called
Listen
    Or defeat will meet you soundly

Just this, recent
        I realize the hollowness is not permanent
In this
        I weigh my vision
        To the void
Tired from the pain
Not to fill a hole
        But fulfill my soul
My all journeys with you
Our journey onward
        Three rosebuds
Fallen and caught
        Catchers do keep
Given
        Each other
In love
        We reap
Kiss the womb
        Of great potential
Eye to eye
        With the woman
        Who delivers me
It is the first time
        Another has seen
        My innate marvels
I see you too
And how adored
        Is that translation
        Whispered back
Time to time
        We must part
        From our embrace
Until when?
Realize a difference
        Between here and Heaven

*

Vision impaired to
    The ruins we knew
Doubtful due to
    Truths we misconstrue
I hoped you wouldn't forget
    The tomb
I hoped you wouldn't forget
    My company
In the big wide plain
    Things look all alone
Stay by my side
    I will show you home
Understand now
    So one can love now
It's the dust that
    Shows your past
It's your waste that
    Attracts the rats
My swollen feet mock surprise
Seldom surprised
    Always appalled
Journey for cure
    Healed along the way

*

You can't walk where
      He did walk
He can't sing when
      You did
You couldn't believe
      You were shown up
      By just one kid
Watches oceans crumble
      By his feet
Waits 'til blue sky turns black
Suddenly he isn't so big
Suddenly he isn't so
Salt water swells
      To the knees
The tide pulls out
      Sky turns red
The tide will bring me
      Back again
Like it always does

*

Fifty years before my first
Were my precious words preceded?
    Dwindle I to apathy accursed
These words of diction
    Beset so long ago
These doubts silence thought
        Never to reach modern minds
        Lay to rot, negate conviction
All goodness need renew
If seek you, truth
        Then seek, renew
Love is but dead
        Without each day, a resurrection

*

I stumble
        Weak and weary
A blade that lost its edge
Grind to sharpen
By the profession of thinking clearly
Id is in the rats in the race
66 channels
        Nothing is on
66 newspapers
        One opinion
Explain the inane reasoning
I bleed much more
        When I know I should not have
        Taken the chance
And so I
        Feel unwelcome in my room
Keep the pilot light lit
        Come tomorrow
Come tomorrow
Not to the know the
        How or when

*

The converse of wretched agony
    Is not ecstasy
It is
    Righteous suffering

*

Hand has lost warmth
    Bundle now in this season
In my earlier time
    I saw spontaneous joy
Free- open
Time was intoxicated
Feel this pain
    I am alive
Absorb this rain
    I will survive

*

Oh, hark!
    A mark of incense
Oh, hark!
    A spot of light
Raised, my dermis
Tasted, blood
Chiming of bells
    Pay the toll
    I cross the bejeweled bridge
Echoes reverberate in my chest
I smell the candles burning
And then
    Ingestion consumes my rest

*

How coarse
    Those tender lips
How bitter
    Those sweet nothings
Deceptive intent
    Sways the literal
Disdain stays both hearts

*

To improve upon the young,
    Slow them
    Into contemplation
To improve upon the old,
    Hasten them
    Into desire
All are afflicted
    Of the young and old
Put to question your self practice
    Cease to do it for a time
It is not a question of in or out
    Rather, entrance through
    By way of sword or key

*

Choose the fires to extinguish
We may have not sparked this one
        But we have neglected
"You mean this metaphorically?"
No
It is real
"Physically extinguish?"
Not always
It is not physical
        At most times
This urgency is much appreciated
        Yet undervalued
The world is wondrous
        When considered with divine
implication

*

The bones of the young
So pristine
Broken through trials
When aligned
And healed
The fusion is stronger than inception

*

Dead on arrival
Playing devil's advocate
    With a proud shield and cynical sword
Add confusion to the understood
    Façade of self confusion
Play the harp, so gentle, demon

*

Woe to thee
Who revel-
    The violation
And weep
    With the punishment
There may be two
    Similarly afflicted
But blessed be the ashamed one
    For righteousness still dwells within
you

*

Wrought tears
    Did this
    Tempest of the mind
The reign
The reign
Flood my mind
Drown my ability
Fantasize about not needing
    The keys
Neglect
    There would be not a lock
Two paths
    One of push
    One of letting go
Ponder where you would
    Be headed
Fact remain
    Your death at stake

*

Truth is right
Yet strive not to be right
But in truth
Argue aspects of truth
As you understand
But listen
All good teachers are students
Humbly, you could be wrong
In humility, you are right

*

Progressive thought
    And accountability to self
This is how a master is born
A master passes on lesson
    To those open to learning
"Is not that cheating them
    Out of their own experience?"
No
That is how a student
    Raises to heights above their own
master
This is how a master is made

*

Is not the intelligence
　　Of the world
So dependent upon
　　The intelligence
　　Of the processor?
I had a near life experience
　　I want you to come with me
What extraordinary phenomena
　　So present outside
Is threefold within you
Something to pursue
　　Inside you, throughout life
How then can expectation lie
　　In conceptualizing another
　　Let alone the celestial?
Yet leave not alone the celestial
Leave not alone your sister and brother
Quiet contemplator
　　Witness to the truth
The light may reflect
　　Or shine through

*

A shadow
    Not darkness, but a remnant of light
I am Shadow Catcher
I know about the fifty pound halo
    Such duty from conscience
Referenced not so much serpentine waters
    As decision without witness

Puff prayer pipe
    Smoke offered incense
Serenity enter lungs, in your breath
Peace past your lips
    Evacuate plight and anxiety
Enter a poverty, emptied
    Hungry for justice
Claim sanctuary
    From your
    Heart's war
The spectrum of humanity
    Ranges us
    From utmost wretched
To redemptive glorious
    Most beautiful
Angels envy us
    Though sin not of Cherubim
Sing so
    Seraphim
I beseech your aid in my endeavor
    To be human

*

Under the wreckage
        Of a human storm
Low day of reckoning ensues
Cursed for cursing
        My Freudian tongue
I have traveled, asunder
        Darkly regarded
For good reason
        In good judgment
For I played foolish
        Confused mercy in my life
        For reward

My shadow takes a stance
    As the sun is behind me
Save myself as you avalanche
    Down the mountain
But if you reach for me
    As will I go
I will let my limbs tell me
    How far
We are all refugees
    In need of our homeland
You cannot tell me
    The bird will not fly another way
Offer seed
    And watch attention pay
It is late
    For the ones without rest
I forgive
    But I cannot forget
A lion lurks in the heather
Let loose your heart
    Mind rational defense
Redirect to your soul
    And on sole you recover the bounty

*

Curse not your enemies
    If you are good
    As you believe to be
Bless your enemies
    They will curse themselves
We are weary of our own fault
In modernity we put our sin
    On the necks of the innocent
Through our derision
    We access the escape
Forty follies
    Lain upon
    Slain in public
Avoid these faults
    In tremor times

*

"The past is gone"
Is it now?
Your chronic disease revisits
   Your memory haunts
   Of past abuse
We wrestle masked foes with ominous
names
A career ensues
   With broken bones and pins
Clear revelation of such pursuits
   A blessing to end
   As a schizophrenic masquerade

*

Ever yet the obedient student
        Impatience resides
Wearily I mock praised objects
        Teach me gold, paint, metal, wood,
teach
Manipulated into forms
        The substance is constant and fulfills
its purpose
        Like a soulful slave, making tyrants of
hands
I thieved what is gifted
Now to open my eyes
        From being a dependent ingrate
Impatience versus gratitude, I turn
Thankful for the lesson
        I search for the teacher
Certainly not the object
        Concurrent epic
Certainly not I, the receiver
I thank the author

The unconcerned
Have been dis-concerned
Curious scientists we are born
Pursuant past our undeveloped eye
For this night
This wine, evident on my breath
Has taken me to a place
Ironically focused, concerned with
significance
A time appropriate
To take off my spectacles to see
A time when guttural voices
Become tuning forks
Outside myself
Outside controlled manipulations
How eager our senses when
Calmed
Collected
Silenced
Without sedation
How attuned the ear then
To identify the drop of a pin
How affirmed the hungry tongue
To the grain of the earth
As I go about this earth
A stumbling fool
In attempts to talk
I mumble
In attempts to do
I bumble- without hindrance
Anxiety abounds
So then time passes quicker through me
Incongruent with the truth

The arsenic will be placed
    In a cool drink
    On a hot day of turmoil
Mistake not summer as
    The sole season of embrace
Autumn softens a parched heart
And spring flowers flow
    From winter snow
The beginning of the year
    Is the birth
Born at the end
    I build from what we have
    Come to know
My fruit is then of autumn
    When often spring for others
    Lest it be my fall
    Because that is my time
I have once felt you
    Reopen my eyes to your splendor
I have not a stance
    Opposed to sitting
Nor do I sit on a stance
Harvest, celebrate, sleep
    In due time

*

All desire love and uniqueness
To be special
Selfishness disguised as self efficacy
Disquieted by injustice
Your trip is your own
A lover moment to moment
Oh, Statue of Liberty can you
Reach above those capitalizing
On the vulnerable
And on those socializing
To take fortitude from the people?
Speak not a word ill-tempered
Permissive upon debauchery's
dismissal
Hot air of humanity sinks
Deep into stale psyches
Strip away fear
Peal away soft comfort
And what you have is your core
Above water
Above ground
Above Ellis
Reach high, her light

*

We are so prone
        To take
And yet if we take
        The time
We would see
        That so much is out there
More than we
        Can receive

*

Able to recognize good will
    Racism
    Prejudice
    Discrimination
Sift, don't sour
I have been down
    These streets
    They shouldn't profile doubt
Stuck on the stoop
    Stay where their momma say
They rhyme
    With the same words
    They rhyme
It is so unbecoming
    Soon they become
    Contempt

Regurgitate pulse of others
    They- beaucoup trife
Katrina take your boy out of Nola
    No taking Nola out your boy
I haven't been rigged with rage
    My war drum
    Did not reverberate
Discovered their vertebrae
    Had no nerve
    Their spine no muscle
Recognize difficult challenge
    Not to roll with majority tide
    Not to polarize in minority pride
Contra flow
Able to recognize good will
    Peace of strength

*

Leave it to man
    To meander
    So aimlessly
To lose all purpose
    Wrapped up in pleasures
Animals fall prey
    When stagnant
Then must we ask
    What is our predator?

*

Desirous to be past
    Our struggles
And having obtained fortune
Let us be present minded
Fight for peace
    Call for silence
Live each day as it is your first
    Without desperate scramble
For we are on both sides
    Of fortune and struggle

*

Duty of conviction:
Measure the accountability
And deliver access
To the masses

*

The "Oh" looks like "Eee"
    And the "Eee" then like "El"
Assuredly, your hole looks like Hell
Lo, Leo up high
Lift your eyes
    And your recovery nigh
Some things are wrong for some
    But not for others
Some things are wrong for all
Some things are all-right
    But other things right for none
It is not your right to decipher
    But you're obligation
Step forth with this designation

*

Simmer…
    Simmer
Glitter, glide
A fish of a new tide
Play and piddle
    You're going to get burned
Stutter, sputter
Dimmer…
    Die

*

I

Oft plots granted to
    A fictional government
    To the persuasive storyteller
Feign disdain of tyranny
    Though oppose deposing tyrants
And what are these useful words
    Without service paid
    By scholars put to use
May my reputation be incurred
    As those favored words
    In so many eulogy
One must bid
    To do anything
A ship is set upon water
    As well as its sail and sailor
Be on deck or course astray

II

One day upon a hundred
It was no suckling-hunger
    But my forgotten, stooping effort
Revealed, rare breed
    Becoming a lasting namesake
I bear in both hands
    A private bounty for you
At what we grab
    We cannot grasp
Take only what is needed
We tire and toil ourselves
    In small minded endeavors
Between our grounded dreams severs

*

III
Saved by our eclectic bid
    That caught the eye looking
To the dry mangrove
    Temple of Ta Prohm
To honor ancient roots
    In contemporary time
    A vain foundation
If to find fountain of youth
    Behold
    The purgative flaming fountain

Early on I discovered
　　With anecdotal evidence
Truth more apparent
　　In the witnessing of avoidance
　　Than in approachment
The disparagement of food
　　So I fed the little duck
　　Of the big flock
Yes the dawn displayed
　　All in front of me
Though my eyes out of focus
　　Persevered to squint
The names came to me
　　Purpose shot through me
Until the titles were told to me
For that previous moment
　　I absorbed prior
　　To permeating

I stumbled upon a stool
    In the dark
    That I placed there myself
I was angered
If for the stool placed
    Self centered retreat
If for the pain
    I succumb to self-pity
If for myself
    Stumble upon accountability

In their proliferation
    The most robust rat
    Is the quickest
The most robust dog
    Is alpha
The robust sheep
    Is favored
But the most robust snake
    Is a cannibal
Be not a consumer of self
Look inward
    Only to attune
    To the expanse of Truth
Break free of your breed

*

The eternal chases me
    Like a father chasing
    His gleeful child
Though now, I forgot the game
A hunting that haunts me now
    When I ceased play
Became weary with poor stamina
Let my thoughts be akin to the words
    Calm the trite hysteria
Disenchanted by drug induced Oracles
I will callous my hands
    In these brief moments
    For an opus
This house of quality
    Only by earned merit
A power which induces
    Not revelry
    But responsibility

*

Ethereal promises arise from doubt
Evaporate from truth pursuant
Unconscious, we are persuaded
One can only fully accept
What one understands

*

Be like the fire
    Consumed and consuming
Desolating that which is rubbish
    Death for new life
Be like the water
    Quench and flow
    And cooler than the
    Environments surrounding
Be like the wind
    Sower of seeds
Be like the rock
    Solid, stabilizing
Internal rhythm vibrate
All this within your being

*

All inhabitants
    Born of goodness
    . Have slight faith
This element enough
    For us to quest for more
And in the end
    Faith is all we have
In killing another
    We accept death proliferating
    Bond exterminated
Likewise, if to embrace life
    Recognize own iniquities
    And pardon
Proceed with pardoning, good shepherd
    Around you life resounds
Be thankful for your meal
    Ushered by the hounds
And for all you hold dear
    Ability to protect
Beseech pardon for missteps
    And you step on holy ground

*

Be it darkness or bright
    Both render one without sight
When engaging outside our element
In seeking sight
    Overcome the differentials
The flow of smoke shows
    Where the wind goes
And at its tail
    You can trail the impetus burn
Olly olly, follow it back home
    Or folly, indicate
    Your enemy

*

Worship in the beat
    Of swollen temples
Contentious bellies churn
Stomping feet of acclaimed rebels
    Such governments never settle
We take in more energy than we expend
Repressions converted to depressions
    And our economies sour
Internal quarrel turns plural
    Ripe was the hour
Failed at invoking vocation
Buffalo hunt
    Would give what one needs
    And one keeps what one received
    Cannot seize without chase

*

Madness abounds
   Burning blazing
Caught within an hour of eternity
This vibrancy rising
   Recognized as content-breaking
Redefinition of you
   But I heard your glory songs bashing
Any condemnation of a group by any one
   A scourge on society
Scorch with desire
   Trail blazer
Economies of size
   Moral inflation led to moral
bankruptcy

*

Got a postcard from Vedder
    Says he's at the Taj Mahal
You know, it's funny
    This world seems so small
Sent the postcard to Portland
    Where he did a show
Lost the postcard, now
    All I have is a
Paper memory

*

Smoke- living receipt
Fire erupts from smoldering debris
Where I discarded the ashes
I still made it out with my life
So in the end, I end up ahead

*

When tempted to quit
    Remind yourself of what it means
"I have given more than any other"
"I can give no more"
"Nothing is worth this"
A good heart objects

*

That act of blessing
    Superior to I
That act of love
    Greater than I
How blessed
    For I'm able to bestow

*

Coach called
    He replaced the receiver

*

When discovering
    A lesson to share
Do not number them
    Lest you assign value
Priority kept
    According to
    Deficiency of student

*

Rights infringe upon
Other rights
And every opinion
Is oppressive
What is left is weighed

*

Perhaps God's greatest
        Weakness
Is us
We personify the wicked wicks
        In crooked candle sticks
Carry on, carry on
        Like some Bristol hum
We brim with confidence
        We- all on our second day
        Of school

*

Evil transforms
Use
    Into misuse

*

The sky is blue
    Because it looks down upon
    All of humanity

*

One may state someone
Is a certain label
It may be accurate
But it is never the conclusion
Pursuit of that feeling
Is oft the problem

*

The line between my truth and lie
Is Heaven and I
That lie is the distance between
Heaven and I
Depart from estrangement, enter

*

There is a man here
     I figured I'd never see again
At the time
     He assured me
     I could never say never
I greet him now
     But his memory does not recall
     It will never recall me
I'll never see that man again

*

There is much relief
In exhaustion
Toil has taken all
I refer not to the rest
But the aspect of having
No other momentary concern

*

In lessons in love
People often want a receipt
    Before buying in
    To trust self abandon
A receipt cannot be rendered
Lest the lesson
    Be for not

*

What is longer?
A transformative day
Or
A minute of ego-babble?

*

Baptized by the cemetery
Shalom
Significant for the city
    Than in a small town
If not blood,
    What makes the namesake wake?
Identity is not
    In recognizing what one is not
It draws the lines that make your shape
The theory remains theory
    And minds stay myth
Yet all these things
    Are hope and faith and you
    Renewed

*

Much like the value of sand
    Of an hour glass
      Is in the purpose of each grain
Such are we
We are the shore
    Of something great

*

What distinction in race have we?
We all,
    Between the whites of our eyes
    And our black pupil
Containing the color spectrum

*

Aid in diverting my eyes
　　Before I cease to see debauchery
So that I do not fail
　　To see it in practice
I shall rejoice my tribulations
For recognition not only
　　In temperance
But in the death of all that dwells
　　In my heart that should not
Be it that anything worth bearing on mind
　　Is weightily leaning on my skull
I have no right to anger
Like a disgruntled child
　　Who is in need of slumber
For my wakeful hours have soured

*

When a dark day of pain
        Is met with rain
You may notch it a sorrow, and
        Lament it's cold, dark outcome
Better to rejoice
        Fully live
        This moment
With the lifeblood of crops
        Cleansing stale urban facades
This is not invitation
        To turn frown to smile
The smile is present in deceit
        Present with assumption
        Before the disturbance of reality
Nervous smiles serve all
        In the face of strangers
Such things are frivolous
Freed from that
        Rejoice in the vast composition
There is that ultimate chance
        To turn without crop or cleansing
What is the opportunity for yourself
        And for those around you

*

We are all uncertain in experience
And contemplation
It is the glimmer of perfection
Of something supreme
That makes the faithful

*

Dark figures in the distance
To what do I attribute?
    The distance between us
    Obscured mindset
    Accounting what got us here
    To what is happening
    Perceptional affect
    Special effect
Fault my vision to the clouds, rain, both
If dark figures becoming forefront
Right in front
    Belated action dispatches me

*

People are looking
    To fix
    For a fix
    To be part of the fix
Own the city
Not by building count
But by the hearts of the people

*

What we need is a prudent purveyor
A fingerless wine
    Won't touch you
Useless in panic
Like a kettle
    Whistling before the heat
Do with distinction
Abandon the process

*

My weaknesses
    They overcome me
    They are stronger than me
My strengths
    Weaker than me
    Inflate me
If only to use the strength
    Overcome the conceit

*

"Know it by heart"
        Does not say much
How properly acquainted
        Are we
        To our own heart?

*

I read an acclaimed book
About
The greatest of journeys
And discovered
That it must be read again

*

Somewhere before the
      Precipice of relativity
Understanding the limits of my scope
But discarding the scope
      Leaves one without measure
Challenging my personal
      Paradigm
Is the wellspring to
      Revelation

*

One should take no heed
    From a quack doctor prognosis
Over preventative
Medicine
But if that quack
    Says duck
One should duck

*

Allow myself joy in my labor
So it gives birth to life
In which I toiled and suffered
That I may be present
In the suffering
Grateful for before the labor
My troubles were greater
May I be delivered upon that day
Among those hours

*

This world without me
    A darker place
    For a time
Change is always in order
If not your thought
    Change is in that order
Will I be
    In the hearts of mankind
Perhaps on the lips
Relevant enough to travel
    From evoked hearts
Provoking eager lips?

*

We chased the titles
     And subjects
All the while
The importance was
     Much more delicate
To you I dedicate
     The predicate

*

Looking up
    To atmosphere
There, in my sky,
    You are, starlet
Where is my representation?
Right near
There, the counterbalance

*

Throwing pearls
    To swine
Putting stock
    In iniquities
Not in giving someone in
    A poverty
    A chance
Poised when depleted

*

Taught in a glass-room
For immediate influence
Contribute to the
    Current trajectory
Young minds, rife ability

*

In significance
By population
In time
We are but one drop
    In the ocean
If we do not join
    We are a difference of two drops
    Becoming part of the restrictive forces
Consider our influence
    We are ten drops
Ripple effect
Consider the influences
    Passed to those we have affected
We are a tributary

*

Throughout this life
        Home comings abound
Building up, up, up through life
        But come trouble
        Evacuate through the bottom floor
But through no prodigal self assurance
        Serves me now
I have come home to die
        Outside resources offer nothing now
Pets wander away to pass
        Now I wander in
Oh how long have I been out
Returning now with tattered bounties

*

To appoint
    It takes an insider
To anoint
    It takes an outsider

*

Delusional
　　And other ways
　　To paint your sky
Are we just as the waves
　　Crashing down on ourselves?
The most treacherous waters
　　Come from what one conducts
Streaming from eyes
　　Projecting deficiencies
Loss of sight

*

Economic seer
   One who
Keeps all
    Accountable

*

One's body grows
But in the process
Diverging between
    Head and feet
Furthering the gap
    Between concept and consummation

*

Pausing to recognize this burning ember
 My hand floats smoke
Ghosts that connect the present of
 What is
To the past of
 What was
To disassemble the structures
 Among the ancient trees
 To be placed in the forest
Up top a crow's nest
 Swishing branches in the night winds
 Reminiscent of perpetual tides
These hands grasp clubs, and arrows,
 And bows, and pipes, pencils,
 And fortification
Both what we fight with
 And what we fight for
To step outside one's self
 Then to convey the sacred
Hierarchy is necessary to facilitate
No place between artist, muse, and art
 Not between sides of a battlefield.

*

All ideas are oppressive
Defending against the contrary

Dispel your beliefs
    Witness small semblances
Small gradients point vastly
Beauty is the beginning
The start of every relationship
It draws us
    So we draw it
Be not afraid of advancing discovery
    Mystery is unobtainable

*

Is it not
    So possible to contrive
A conjecture so irrelevant
That it provokes discussion and
    Is provocative

*

It is not enough to be human
    "It is my nature"
Not a call to be superhuman
    Calling to be supernatural
To rise to the occasion
    Rise above
One must prepare in ordinary time
    In lieu of that occasion
If reserved to go by whim and whistle
It will get darker
    Than any night underground
Just because Auschwitz snow is not cold
    Should not comfort you

*

Defend the defenseless
Save the senseless
Afford them at least
One more moment
To come to realize
Each moment antiquates the next
Now you are acting out
What you have scripted long ago
Back then, seemed so apropos
Comfortable taking stations
In times of war and depression
Do not know where you stand
With your own turmoil
Once the noise drops

*

Frightful creatures feel the most fear
Intoxicants are inept oracles
Nightmare recalled a memory
Insincerely seeking seers
It's a bella sera
It's a bella vie
Crossed the konditorei
Sip a spell on some coffee
Hitched a ride upon a troika
Perception, preparation
Poise
Faith in hopeful love
Landed on a syzygy

*

We are a world of wars
    The wars begin from within
Muted voices to implore
    We are to blame for our myopic view
In time of distress
    Baby looks for one
    The mother of all inventors
When did the worship
    Cease to be holy?
When did the mystery
    Lose its mystique?
In the vast immensity
    Celebrating more unknown than
known

*

For those who need
Syllables' inundation
     To grant attention
I'll leave you
To the prose

I
Being with you
    Milk and honey rhapsody
Demystify infatuation with you
Then enters love
And by you
    I am mystified again
Mature as art
    Like fine wine
Without love,
    We:
    Aged vinegar
Flavors arise regardless
    Via time
Disrupt the onslaught of self destruction
    And choose, daily, to grow young
together
We grow and welcome this third entity
    This love
    Binding us
How about that endeavor
    To decipher the language
    To study the art, to
Become the connoisseur
Squander one's self when
    Giving to the emergent

II
Emergent tremors betray
    Leading to quakes that decimate
Is not what you seek in the 2nd
    What you sought in the 1st?
Parting from this life together

*

Without you
    Then my being would be departed
Your softest safest spot invaded
    Into your heart
The endeavor devoured me,
    Consuming my all
    Assimilating into your all

For true love is between two
    To split is to divide that love
    Unrequited delusion
I have been deconstructed
    Now redefined
You gave me heart
    I was intoxicated with purpose
Now not detecting much flavor,
    Merely maintaining in this era of
neglect
Am I my own single admirer, nurturing my
wounds
No consultation to the third entity
My question turns me rhetorical
    Answering self, soliloquy
    "Seek another?"

III
I hold you as you weep
    With your sorrow
Your tears roll down my cheek
Your tears become my tears
The opposite of love
    Is the guise of love
What is the purpose of the wayward glance?
    A quick read, for what information?
Instinct over intent

*

Something other than you
Driving you
Body facing me
Face turned aside
Effort doubtless partner- appreciation, love,
and care
You may like flowers, but have mercy
Your starving garden
You December like frost
End this wicked season
The flowers produced
From that entity created between us
The communication, the connection spills
Confusion sets
Why can she no longer see?
Show her sight again

IV
On hypocritical loins
One leaps to another anybody
All the while expending that effort
That investment squandered
Can never have that dirty laundry laundered
Every action leaves an indelible mark
Be it pure or stain
Must we reconvene in our minds and remind
our eyes?
Expose its farce:
"Once lost, forever lost"
Not to reconvene, but to convene again and
again
Anew and always anew
In those first days, when mystery marked
our ways
Unfamiliar to one another's days

*

And so there was that union
That crept in our hearts
Out of our eager eyes
Slept in our bellies
Life is hard, love softens
    Love hardens when mismanaged
    Through self preservation
I connect with her eyes
    Then I approach the rest of her being
We take this recognition of each other and
cradle it
Considering the great struggle
Coming home from battle
So comforting to return to the sole duty of
rest
At home to the arms
    Invited by the heart
Binding self to obligation frees me
I am fidelity
    I have faith in us
Every pearl has its price
    What ransom more worth while?

V
Physical love is accounted through
acquisition
Amalgamation accounts for the spiritual
So to love in this world
    We acquire through coming together
    Both giving of self
As love has restored us as nebula stars,
Our obligation-
    To restore the light when it wanes
Restorative, ever new
    Awake in this

*

Glorious morning
Patiently your passion grows
Energized into the art
And it draws your love closer
More than glittery and glistening, she is
luminous
There is a physical manifestation of our
third entity
Our love, our life
Replete, let our brackish spirits rise
Through our time together
Your name changes with me
First "enigma, desire"
Eventually "destiny"
And through so many more "Lover"
All these and more
By the day
This final chapter
Is the first of ours
In the break of every day
Turn toward your touch
Sprinkle petals without thought much
The rapturous fortune
Let us be the everlasting cadre of love
I pledge all this forever and
Ever Afterglow

www.ingramcontent.com/pod-product-compliance
Lightning Source LLC
Chambersburg PA
CBHW021156020426
42331CB00003B/90